T0131713

I'd like to thank the following people for helping with this book:
Tracy Anglada for support and editing, Hannah, Jessica, & Matthew
for inspiration and illustrations, Grandma Bev, and my husband Jeff.

Order this book online at www.trafford.com
or email orders@trafford.com

Most Trafford titles are also available at major online book retailers.

 www.trafford.com

**North America & international**
toll-free: 1 888 232 4444 (USA & Canada)
fax: 812 355 4082

Our mission is to efficiently provide the world's finest, most comprehensive book publishing service, enabling every author to experience success. To find out how to publish your book, your way, and have it available worldwide, visit us online at www.trafford.com

Because of the dynamic nature of the Internet, any web addresses or links contained in this book may have changed since publication and may no longer be valid. The views expressed in this work are solely those of the author and do not necessarily reflect the views of the publisher, and the publisher hereby disclaims any responsibility for them.

Any people depicted in stock imagery provided by Getty Images are models, and such images are being used for illustrative purposes only.
Certain stock imagery © Getty Images.

ISBN: 978-1-4120-5425-6 (sc)

Print information available on the last page.

Trafford rev. 10/22/2019

Hi! My name is Robert. I have bipolar disorder. I used to think that meant I was part polar bear, but Mom says it's because my feelings to up, up, up, and down, down, down.

The doctors call it bipolar because your feelings
go to the top and the bottom of the world. I call it roller
coaster because my feelings go up and down, around
and around, at the speed of sound!
Let's take a look...

When other kids are happy, you can tell by the smiles on their faces or the twinkle in their eyes. When I'm happy, I hug everyone real big, I start giggling, and I feel like doing back flips! Mom and Dad call it bouncing off the walls. Dr. Janet calls it silly, giddy, & goofy.

My teacher says one of the best things about having me in class is how excited I get about learning—it makes school more fun. I learned some really exciting things about penguins! Emperor Penguins can be 4 feet tall! Daddy penguins stand for 2 months balancing an egg on their feet and they don't even get to eat!
Tomorrow, I'm even going to remember to raise my hand!

Have you ever asked your mom for candy at the grocery store and had her say "no"? The last time it happened to me, I couldn't get the candy out of my head, I wanted it so much!

I got so mad!! I even threw the bag of candy at my mom. We had to leave the store. Mom calls it a rage when I do that. She says I can't go shopping with her for a while, until I feel better. I feel bad because I embarrassed my mom in front of all those people.

When the lights go out at night, I don't just get a little scared,
I get terrified! I can't help it. My brain goes in fast motion,
like a movie in fast forward and I can't stop it.

Dad says that the scary things in books and movies aren't real.
My mom rubs my back and puts on soft music. That helps.

Other times, I'm just plain cranky. Every thing irritates me—the seams in my socks, my sister's voice, and the smell of food cooking. And, if you make me wait for anything, it feels like my head is going to pop!

Mom tells me to go outside, ride my bike around the block a few hundred times, or take a bath. That usually helps me feel better.

Sometimes, I get so frustrated! Like when I'm tying my shoes and they're too tight, then too loose, and I just can't get it right! Mom says I can't throw my shoes when I get frustrated because I could put a hole in the wall or hurt someone.

Dad says to take a deep breath and ask for help. It's hard to
think when I'm frustrated, but I'll keep trying.
Practice makes progress!!

This morning, I panicked in school. I couldn't find my homework
and all I could think was "I'm going to flunk math! I'm so stupid!"

I took some deep breaths so I could think. Then I remembered—
Mom told me to put it in my agenda so I wouldn't lose it!
Wow, that was close!!

When I'm depressed, I feel sad and lonely. I can't tell you why,
but I just want to curl up in my bed and pull the blanket
over my head. It feels like the end of the world, and
like no one cares about me.

To feel better, I look at a picture of my family hugging me and I remember that people love me. Besides, we're having a pizza party at school tomorrow! Sometimes, nothing makes me feel better—Dr. Janet says that's when I need to tell my parents or her and get help.

Last week, the kids in the neighborhood were playing kick-
ball in my front yard. I got an out and a kid on my team called
me "stupid". I hate those kids! I didn't want to cry in front of
them, so I pushed him. He fell down and scraped his knee. The
kids were all mad at me. Who cares?!!

My sister told the kids that, just like loud noises and strong
smells really bother me, my feelings get hurt easily too. I said I
was sorry and they said they wouldn't call me names anymore.
Boy, do I love my sister, and I'm glad I still have friends!

At karate class, we have to learn self-control. It's hard because karate is exciting and I feel like I'm in a Power Ranger™ movie. But, in real life, you can hurt someone if you get out of control. So, I wait my turn and only do what the teacher says I can do.

Honesty    Respect    Self Control    Self Discipline

In school, I practice self-control by keeping my hands to myself in line and using walking feet instead of being Spider-man™ in the halls. It's not as much fun, but, safety first!!

Yesterday, I got a 100 on my first spelling test of the year! Wait  till I tell my mom and dad! They're going to be so proud of me! Later, at lunch, a kid called me names, but I counted to 10 and ignored him. Know what? Now I'm proud of myself!

I don't like having bipolar disorder, but I can't change that. I also don't like having to take all those pills, but, the bad nightmares have gone away and they help me have more good days. Dad says a lot of kids have things wrong with their bodies, like asthma and diabetes, and they have to take medicine and be careful too. I guess I'm not the only one.

Mom and Dad say that bipolar disorder is just a part of who I am,
not all of who I am. They tell me they love me and that they
always will. Dr. Janet says it's only been a little while since
doctors knew that kids could have bipolar disorder.
She says they're working hard to help us feel better.
In the meantime, I'll just keep trying my best.

Printed in the United States
By Bookmasters